MEGA
Colouring

Parragon

Bath · New York · Cologne · Melbourne · Delhi
Hong Kong · Shenzhen · Singapore

Husky pup Everest zooms down Jake's Mountain on her rocket-powered snowboard.

Skye is waiting to greet her best pal
Everest in Adventure Bay.

At the Lookout, Rubble and Chase are
getting ready to race. Ready, set, go!

Skye has perfected an amazing new trick.
Marshall thinks it's PAWsome!

It's not all work and no play.
Marshall and Rocky have fun playing ball together.

The PAW Patrol are always ready to help the citizens of Adventure Bay. Just yelp for help!

Katie runs the pet parlour with the help
of her charming but mischievous cat, Cali.

Katie helps to keep the pups happy and healthy!

Ryder gets a worried call from Katie. She needs the PAW Patrol's help – Cali is stuck in a tree!

Ryder gathers the PAW Patrol together at the Lookout.

This is a job for fire-pup Marshall.
He can use his ladder to rescue Cali.

The PAW Patrol is on the job!

Marshall climbs up to rescue Cali,
but a rung on his ladder snaps. Uh oh!

Luckily Ryder knows the perfect pup to help.
Rocky always finds the right thing to solve the problem.

"Don't lose it – reuse it!"

Rocky finds a broom handle to fix Marshall's ladder.

Marshall zooms up to collect Cali,
then carries her back down. *Whoosh!*

What good pups!
Ryder rewards them for doing a great job.

The PAW Patrol discovered their newest member in the jungle – meet Tracker!

Tracker's Pup Pack is fitted with a handy multi-tool.
He's ready for anything!

Alongside Tracker, the brave pups
work together as the Jungle Patrol.

The pups love their special Jungle Patrol gear.

Tracker uses his super-sensitive hearing
to help the PAW Patrol on their missions.

Ryder is proud of all the pups.
No job is too big, no pup is too small.

Everest helps Marshall practise his snowboarding skills on Jake's Mountain.

Chase gathers sticks to add the finishing touches to Skye's snowman.

Skye and Everest are best friends.
They love playing in the snow together.

Ready, set, get wet! Zuma is always ready to dive in to any water rescue missions.

Ryder and Zuma are going to visit
Cap'n Turbot on the Flounder.

Cap'n Turbot has moored the
Flounder near Seal Island.

Cap'n Turbot and Wally the Walrus are playing hide-and-seek. Can you spot Wally?

Now it's Cap'n Turbot's turn to hide.
Can you help Ryder find him?

Skye is a determined pup – she'll nurture
this tiny plant into a big, strong tree.

Rubble's bucket-arm scoop can carry anything!

Chase gives some little ducklings
a tour of Adventure Bay.

"Why trash it when you can stash it?"
To Rocky, someone else's trash is his treasure.

The PAW Patrol love to have fun in the park.
Pups that play together, stay together!

Rocky zooms down the slide.
Whoosh!

Marshall finds a baby goose waddling around
the Lookout. Marshall names him Fuzzy.

Skye thinks Fuzzy is adorable! "Looks like you have a new Best Goose Friend Forever," she says.

Rocky and Rubble fill a nest with bread
for all the geese to eat.

Marshall fetches a piece of bread for Fuzzy.

Marshall makes a trail of breadcrumbs
for Fuzzy to follow.

Sweet dreams, Marshall and Fuzzy!

It's time for the geese to fly home.
Skye gives Marshall a lift so he can join Fuzzy.

"You're the best goose friend a pup could have," Marshall says. "Bye, Fuzzy!"

Marshall flies back to the Lookout in style!

Great job pups, another successful mission.

They're all good pups!

"It's time for a treat," says Ryder.

Rocky, Zuma and Chase are
playing puppy in the middle.

Marshall is teaching Robo-dog some cool new tricks.

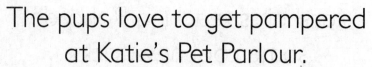

The pups love to get pampered
at Katie's Pet Parlour.

Skye treats herself to a new paw-dicure!

Rubble loves to get covered in mud ...
but he also loves warm bubble baths.

Marshall, Rocky and Chase are playing basketball.

Wow, great shot Marshall!

Rocky passes the ball to Chase.
Boing!

Oh no! As Chase rushes to catch Rocky's pass,
he trips and hurts himself.

Don't worry Chase – Marshall can
use his paramedic skills to help!

Ready for a ruff-ruff rescue!

Marshall activates his X-ray arm
to find out what's wrong with Chase.

All better! "Thanks, Marshall," says Chase.

Ryder is proud of his pups, they always
look out for each other.

Everest's Pup House transforms into
an awesome snowplough!

Cheeky Cali hitches a ride around
Adventure Bay on Rubble's back.

Safety first! Police pup Chase stops traffic
so the ducklings can cross the road.

Rubble and Zuma want to play a game.
What do you think they should play?

Oh no! Some rocks are blocking the train tracks and a train is stuck on the bridge.

The PAW Patrol is on a roll!

Ryder leads the PAW Patrol on their mission.

Construction pup Rubble is perfect for the job.
His bulldozer can scoop the rocks off the track!

Careful everyone – there are pups at work!

Let's dig it!
Rubble clears all the rocks away.

One of the bridge's support beams has cracked
– it needs to be fixed quickly!

Chase finds a tree trunk they can use as a support and secures it with his winch.

Rubble can use his digger to push the beam to the bridge.

Once again the PAW Patrol saves the day!

Best friends make the best team.
Whenever you need the PAW Patrol, just yelp for help!